Alabama

A Buddy Book
by
Julie Murray

ABDO
Publishing Company

VISIT US AT
www.abdopub.com

Published by ABDO Publishing Company, 4940 Viking Drive, Edina, Minnesota 55435.

Copyright © 2006 by Abdo Consulting Group, Inc. International copyrights reserved in all countries. No part of this book may be reproduced in any form without written permission from the publisher. Buddy Books™ is a trademark and logo of ABDO Publishing Company.

Printed in the United States.

Edited by: Sarah Tieck
Contributing Editor: Michael P. Goecke
Graphic Design: Deb Coldiron, Maria Hosley
Image Research: Sarah Tieck
Photographs: Getty Images, Library of Congress, NASA, One Mile Up, PhotoDisc, Photos.com

Library of Congress Cataloging-in-Publication Data

Murray, Julie, 1969-
    Alabama / Julie Murray.
       p. cm. — (The United States)
    Includes bibliographical references and index.
    ISBN 1-59197-660-X
       1. Alabama—Juvenile literature. [1. Alabama.] I. Title.

F326.3.M87 2005
976.1—dc22
                                         2003070813

Table Of Contents

A Snapshot Of Alabama

Alabama is known as the "Heart of Dixie." This is because it is important in the history of the southern part of the United States.

The state of Alabama is where important papers were signed during the American Civil War. These papers said that Alabama and other Southern states were not part of the United States any more. This is also where the Southern government was established during this time.

There are 50 states in the United States. Every state is different. Every state has an official state nickname.

Most of the Alabama region became part of a United States territory in 1798. The United States took control of Mobile during the War of 1812. In 1817, the Alabama territory was created. Alabama became the 22nd state on December 14, 1819.

This is a wetland. Alabama has many different kinds of land.

Alabama has about 51,718 square miles (133,949 sq km) of land. It ranks 29th in size compared to the other states. There are 4,447,100 people living in Alabama today.

Beef cattle and cotton are products of Alabama's farms.

Where Is Alabama?

There are four parts of the United States. Each part is called a region. Each region is in a different area of the country. The United States Census Bureau says the four regions are the Northeast, the South, the Midwest, and the West.

Alabama is in the South region. The weather in this part of the United States is usually warm and humid. Sometimes it gets very hot.

Four Regions of the United States of America

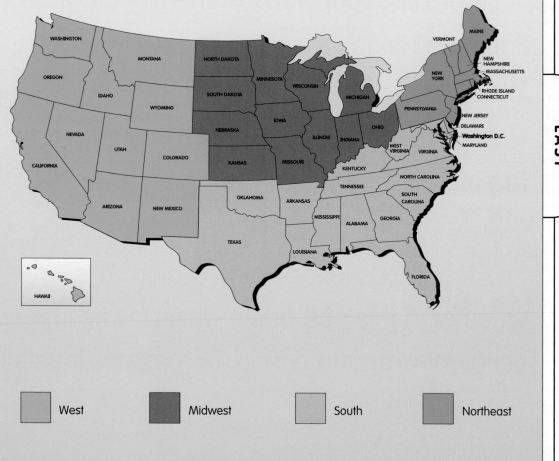

ALASKA

WASHINGTON
MONTANA
NORTH DAKOTA
MINNESOTA
VERMONT
MAINE
OREGON
IDAHO
WYOMING
SOUTH DAKOTA
WISCONSIN
MICHIGAN
NEW
HAMPSHIRE
MASSACHUSETTS
NEW
YORK
RHODE ISLAND
CONNECTICUT
NEVADA
UTAH
NEBRASKA
IOWA
ILLINOIS
INDIANA
OHIO
PENNSYLVANIA
NEW JERSEY
DELAWARE
CALIFORNIA
COLORADO
KANSAS
MISSOURI
WEST
VIRGINIA
VIRGINIA
Washington D.C.
MARYLAND
KENTUCKY
ARIZONA
NEW MEXICO
OKLAHOMA
ARKANSAS
TENNESSEE
NORTH CAROLINA
SOUTH
CAROLINA
MISSISSIPPI
ALABAMA
GEORGIA
TEXAS
LOUISIANA
FLORIDA

HAWAII

West   Midwest   South   Northeast

Alabama is bordered by four other states. Tennessee is north. Georgia is east. Mississippi is west. Florida is south and to the east of the southwestern tip. Also, the Gulf of Mexico is on the southwestern tip of Alabama.

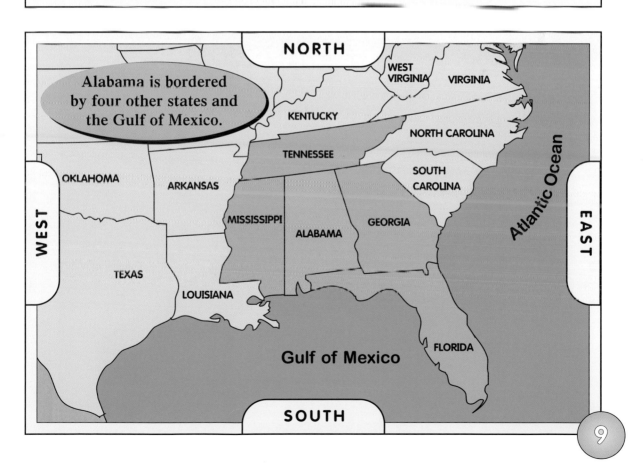

Alabama is bordered by four other states and the Gulf of Mexico.

Alabama

State abbreviation: **AL**

State nickname: The Heart of Dixie

State capital: Montgomery

State motto: Audemus jura nostra defendere ("We dare defend our rights")

Statehood: December 14, 1819, 22nd State

State flag: Adopted in 1895

Population: 4,447,100, ranks 23rd

Land area: 51,718 square miles (133,949 sq km), ranks 29th

State song: "Alabama"

State government: Three branches: legislative, executive, and judicial

Average July temperature: 80°F (27°C)

Average January temperature: 46°F (8°C)

State flower: Camellia

State bird: Yellowhammer

State tree: Southern Longleaf Pine

Cities And The Capital

Montgomery is the capital of the state of Alabama. It is also the second-largest city. Montgomery is located in an area with many farms.

The capitol building is in Montgomery.

Many important events in history happened in Montgomery. This city was the capital of the Southern states for a short time during the Civil War. Also, Montgomery is where the civil rights movement started in the 1950s.

Birmingham became a city in 1871. It started near two railroads. It is in the foothills of the Appalachian Highlands. Today, it is the largest city in Alabama.

Mobile was founded in 1702. It is one of the oldest cities in the United States. It is the third-largest city in Alabama. It is located on Mobile Bay.

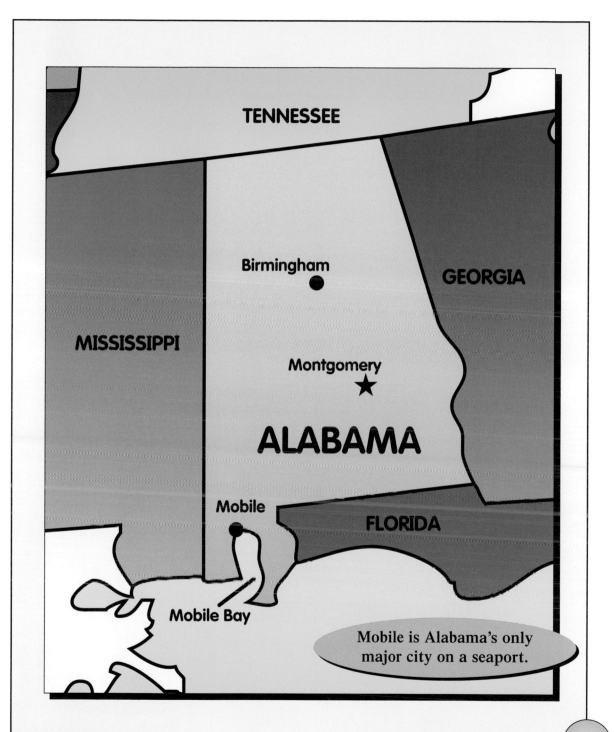

TENNESSEE

Birmingham
●

GEORGIA

MISSISSIPPI

Montgomery
★

ALABAMA

Mobile
●

FLORIDA

Mobile Bay

Mobile is Alabama's only major city on a seaport.

Famous Citizens

Helen Keller (1880–1968)

Helen Keller was born in Tuscumbia on June 27, 1880. She became blind and deaf when she was about one year old. When she was seven, a woman named Anne Sullivan came to be her teacher.

Sullivan helped Keller learn to read and write using Braille. Keller was famous for helping other people who were blind and deaf. She gave speeches and wrote many books.

Helen Keller

Famous Citizens

Jesse Owens (1913–1980)

Jesse Owens was born in Oakville. He was a famous athlete. He was a runner. He won four gold medals in track at the 1936 Olympics. During his career, he set seven world records. In 1976, President Gerald Ford gave him the Medal of Freedom. This is a very important American honor.

Jesse Owens

U.S. Space And Rocket Center

Huntsville is sometimes called "Rocket City, U.S.A." This is because scientists created many rockets in Huntsville. Also, it is home to the U.S. Space and Rocket Center. The U.S. Space and Rocket Center has many exhibits. The world's largest collection of space-related items is there.

The U.S. Space and Rocket Center has many exhibits. Some show famous rockets.

Some of the exhibits include information about astronauts.

Visitors can tour several spacecraft. They can even see one that landed on the moon. This is also where Space Camp for kids happens.

There is a Space Camp at the U.S. Space and Rocket Center. There, people learn about space shuttles.

Battleship Memorial Park

Battleship Memorial Park is located in Mobile. The park is on the waterfront by Mobile Bay. Historic ships and airplanes are displayed there.

The USS *Alabama* is there. This is a battleship. The USS *Alabama* fought in World War II. A World War II submarine is also there. It is called the USS *Drum*.

The USS *Alabama* is located at Battleship Memorial Park.

Alabama Football

Alabama has a history of great college football by two teams. One is the University of Alabama Crimson Tide. The team's **nickname** refers to the school's colors. Crimson and white are the school's colors.

The University of Alabama football team is called the "Crimson Tide."

University of Alabama football started in the 1890s. Many people came to watch the games. The team has won many championships and bowl games since.

Bear Bryant (right) was a famous coach. He coached many great football players including Joe Namath (left).

One of the team's coaches was famous. His name was Paul William Bryant. His nickname was "Bear." He was coach from 1958 to 1982. Bear Bryant was famous because he helped the team win many games. The team won more games than any other major college football team at that time.

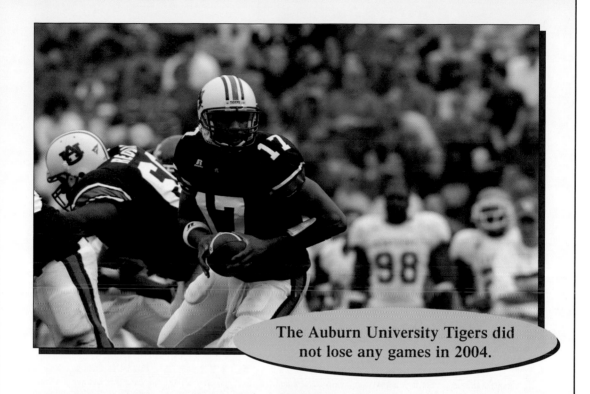

The Auburn University Tigers did not lose any games in 2004.

The other great college football team in Alabama is the Auburn University Tigers. In recent years, they have been among the best teams in the United States. In 2004, the Tigers had a perfect season. This means they won all of their games.

Alabama

1702: The city of Mobile is established by French-Canadian explorers. Mobile is one of the oldest cities in the United States.

People marched together in the fight for civil rights. This march happened in 1965.

1817: Alabama becomes a United States territory.

1819: Alabama becomes the 22nd state on December 14.

1861: Alabama says it is no longer part of the United States.

1866: Electric trolley streetcars run in Montgomery. These are the first electric trolleys in the United States.

1868: Alabama rejoins the United States.

1941: The Redstone Arsenal opens in Huntsville. This is where the United States government made rockets and spacecraft.

1955: Martin Luther King, Jr. starts the civil rights movement in Alabama. He asks African-American people not to ride the bus. This was important because of an African-American woman named Rosa Parks. She was arrested because she did not give up her seat on a Montgomery bus.

1960: George C. Marshall Space Flight Center opens in Huntsville.

2005: Auburn University's football team finishes the season undefeated after beating Virginia Tech in the Sugar Bowl.

Cities in Alabama

Huntsville

Tuscumbia

Oakville

Birmingham

Tuscaloosa

Auburn

★ Montgomery

Mobile

Important Words

American Civil War the United States War between the Northern and Southern states.

Braille a system of writing and printing for blind people.

capital a city where government leaders meet.

civil rights rights for all citizens.

civil rights movement public fight for civil rights.

nickname a name that describes something special about a person or a place.

World War II the second war between many countries that happened from 1939–1945.

Web Sites

To learn more about Alabama, visit ABDO Publishing Company on the World Wide Web. Web site links about Alabama are featured on our Book Links page. These links are routinely monitored and updated to provide the most current information available.

www.abdopub.com

Index